TIMELINES IN SCIENCE

THE
INDUSTRIAL
REVOLUTION

Craig Bou

ROSEN
PUBLISHING

Published in 2025 by The Rosen Publishing Group, Inc.
2544 Clinton Street, Buffalo, NY 14224

Portions of this work were originally authored by Charlie Samuels and published as *The Rise of Industry*. All new material in this edition was authored by Craig Boutland.

PICTURE CREDITS
t=top, b=bottom, l=left, r=right, c=center

Front Cover: Shutterstock: Igor. Golovniov tl, Pedal the Stock tc, Richard Semik tr, Elena Zinenko main.
Inside: Alamy: GL Archive 13, Icom Images 46; iStock: 38b, Peter Bates 18t, Jonathan Maddock 50, RangerX 36, Thinkstock (royalty free TS sub); Photos.com, 7b, 9t, 14, 17b, 18b, 21, 28, 29, 31, 32, 33b, 34t, 37b, 38t, 39, 40, 41t, 47, 48bl, 49, 51, 52b, 58, 59b, 60, 60-61, 61, Tim Ward 9b; Library of Congress: 15, 56; Look and Learn: 42, 44; Public Domain: 11, Olfo Arenius 10, Metropolitan Museum of Art 48t, Museum of the History of France 45, National Biodiversity Center 26, National Portrait Gallery of Sweden; 24, OpenAccess 6, Private Collection 54, Sandon Hall, Stafford Library room/The Yorck Project 56, Uppsala: Stockholm 25, 27; Shutterstock: Martin Bergsma 12, Dja65 33tl, Evereatt 43, Martin Fischer 20, Igor Golovniov 59t, David Hughes 5, J.T. Lewis 52t, Nejron Photo 22, Andejs Polivanovs 17t, Valeriya Repina 34b,, Vaklav 7t, Zhuda 37t; Topfoto: The Granger Collection: 23; Wellcome Images: 57.

All other artwork and illustrations Brown Bear Books Ltd

Cataloging-in-Publication Data

Names: Boutland, Craig.
Title: The industrial revolution / Craig Boutland.
Description: Buffalo, NY : Rosen Young Adult, 2025. | Series: Timelines in science |
   Includes glossary and index.
Identifiers: ISBN 9781499477733 (pbk.) | ISBN 9781499477740 (library bound) |
   ISBN 9781499477757 (ebook)
Subjects: LCSH: Industrial revolution–Juvenile literature. | Inventions–History–18th century–Juvenile literature.
   | Industrial equipment–History–18th century–Juvenile literature. | Transportation engineering–History–18th
   century–Juvenile literature. | Economic history–Juvenile literature.
Classification: LCC HD2321.B68 2025 | DDC 338.0973–dc23

Manufactured in the United States of America

CPSIA Compliance Information: Batch #CSRYA25.
For further information, contact Rosen Publishing at 1-800-237-9932.

Find us on

CONTENTS

Introduction

The scientific developments of the 18th century shaped the modern world, introducing industrialization, mass production, and rapid transportation.

Increasingly, the people who made scientific advances were professionals such as engineers. They saw scientific research as a tool for the advancement of business as well as for the improvement of the world. As always, advances often came through gradual steps. Iron had already been used for many centuries. Early in the 18th century, however, a new way to produce it made it much cheaper. That change was instrumental to developments such as the invention of steam engines, which pumped water from mines, and the building of railroads. Boat transportation also improved, both at sea and with the construction of canal systems to move around the raw materials and manufactured goods of industry. In the countryside, agricultural machines helped farmers to produce more food in order to support the growing populations of towns and cities.

Scientific and Social Changes

The profound changes in transportation and in manufacturing and production created great social change. For the first time, workers were brought together in large factories. Their work was increasingly done on machines, and the things they made were the first examples of mass production. At the end of the 18th century, both the United States and France underwent great political upheaval.

About This Book

This book uses timelines to describe scientific and technological advances from about 1700 to about 1800. A continuous timeline of the period runs along the bottom of all the pages. Its entries are color-coded to indicate the different fields of science to which they belong. Each chapter also has its own subject-specific timeline, which runs vertically down the edge of the page.

Underlying much of the Industrial Revolution was the development of cheaper ways of making iron in blast furnaces. The basic technology is still in use today.

Iron Smelting

Although iron working had been known since early times, iron tools and weapons remained rare until the invention of the blast furnace in about 700 CE.

Great heat (over 1,600°F/900°C) is needed to melt iron from its ore.

TIMELINE
1700–1703

KEY:

Biology and Medicine

Engineering and Invention

Astronomy and Math

1700 German mathematician Gottfried Leibniz founds the Berlin Academy, the first national academy of science.

1700

1701

1701 Italian physician Giacomo Pylarini inoculates three children in Constantinople with smallpox to prevent more serious disease when they are older.

Iron is found in ores. These must be smelted to produce usable metal.

Ironworking spread from ancient Egypt and Anatolia (modern Turkey) to India and China. Ancient Greeks joined blocks of stone with iron bolts. In about 400 BCE, Chinese craftsmen made statues from a type of cast iron. The first blast furnace for iron, the Catalan forge in Spain, is thought to date from about 700 CE.

Developments in England

By the 14th century, England was Europe's main iron-producing country. Waterwheels powered the bellows to produce a continuous stream of air for the blast furnaces, which could produce up to 3.3 tons (3 metric tons) of iron a day. This output required large amounts of charcoal, produced by burning wood. As a result of this activity, most of

This illustration shows workers in a 16th-century blast furnace; one man operates the bellows while the other melts the iron.

1701 English agriculturalist Jethro Tull invents a mechanical seed drill for sowing seeds.

1702 English anatomist William Cowper discovers Cowper's glands in the male reproductive system.

1703 English physicist Francis Hawksbee invents an improved vacuum pump.

1701

1702

1703

1701 English astronomer Edmund Halley produces a map of the world showing magnetic variations.

1703 The Eddystone Lighthouse in the English Channel is washed away in a storm, killing its architect.

Blast Furnace

Metalworkers made a furnace by digging a hole and adding a conical chimney. The furnace was filled with iron ore, limestone, and charcoal, and set on fire. Bellows blasted air through the furnace. The ore changed into metallic iron by the action of carbon monoxide (CO), formed by the action of air on the charcoal (carbon). The limestone helped trap impurities.

Britain's forests were destroyed. Then, in 1709, English iron founder Abraham Darby began using coke (derived from coal) instead of charcoal. Darby's development had a dramatic effect on the production, and uses of cast iron, and cast-iron pans, pots, and kettles soon became commonplace in homes across England, Scotland, and Wales.

Improving the Process

Abraham Darby built his furnaces at Coalbrookdale on the banks of the Severn River in southwest England. In 1742, his son, Abraham Darby II, installed a steam engine to pump water from the river to power the bellows. Then, in 1779, Darby's grandson, Abraham Darby III, used prefabricated cast-iron sections to build a bridge over the Severn River at Coalbrookdale. It is 98 feet (30 m) long and stands 39 feet (12 m) above the water.

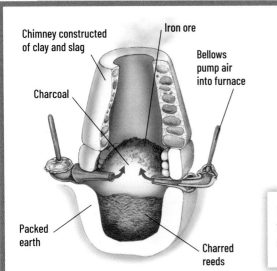

Chimney constructed of clay and slag

Iron ore

Bellows pump air into furnace

Charcoal

Packed earth

Charred reeds

Bellows were used to force air into the furnace. This raised the temperature so that molten iron could form.

TIMELINE

1704–1708

KEY:

Biology and Medicine

Engineering and Invention

Astronomy and Math

Chemistry and Physics

1704 English scientist Isaac Newton publishes his book *Opticks,* about the nature and behavior of light.

1704

1706

1704 Italian clockmaker Nicolas Fatio de Duiller makes a clock with jewel bearings.

1706 English physicist Francis Hawksbee constructs an electrostatic generator.

The bridge at Coalbrookdale was the first major bridge to be made of cast iron. Work started in 1779, and the bridge opened in 1781.

The iron was cast at Darby's foundry. The pieces were bolted together on-site.

The final improvements to the blast furnace came in the 1800s. In Glasgow, Scotland, in 1828, Scottish engineer James Neilson improved its efficiency by sending the air through a red-hot tube to preheat it. The tube was heated at first by a coal fire and later by coal gas, a byproduct from coking furnaces. English inventor Edward Cowper improved Neilson's design in 1857 with his hot-blast stove, which used gases from the blast furnace itself to preheat the air.

1706 Welsh mathematician William Jones introduces the symbol pi for the ratio of the circumference of a circle to its diameter.

1708 German alchemist Johann Böttger invents hard-paste porcelain (previously, porcelain-making was known only to the Chinese).

1706

1707

1708

1707 English physician John Floyer produces a special watch for counting the pulse rates of patients.

1708 Brook Taylor devises a solution to the problem of the "centre of oscillation" important in wave mechanics. It remains unpublished until 1714.

Measuring Temperature

Until the early 1700s, there was no accurate way of measuring temperature. Then Polish instrument maker Gabriel Fahrenheit found a way to measure heat and cold.

One of the most important activities in modern science is measuring temperature. Nowadays we take it for granted that we can swiftly find the temperature of our own bodies, or the air around us. And yet until the early 1700s there was no accurate way of assessing temperature. In 1596, Galileo had devised an instrument we now call a thermoscope. This enabled him to tell whether one thing was hotter or colder than another. But it could not describe what that

Anders Celsius, who invented the temperature scale that bears his name.

TIMELINE
1709–1712

KEY:

Biology and Medicine

Engineering and Invention

Astronomy and Math

Chemistry and Physics

1709 English iron founder Abraham Darby introduces the use of coke for iron smelting.

1709 English physicist Francis Hawksbee describes capillary action, which causes sponges or blotting paper to soak up liquid.

1709

1709 Polish-born Dutch physicist Gabriel Fahrenheit invents the alcohol thermometer and the Fahrenheit temperature scale.

Gabriel Fahrenheit at work devising a thermometer, in a drawing from the 1700s.

Timeline

1596 Galileo invents a thermoscope

1654 The first enclosed thermometer is created in Tuscany, Italy

1714 Fahrenheit makes an enclosed thermometer with mercury inside and a graduated scale

1742 Celsius creates a temperature scale using 100 units

1848 Lord Kelvin creates the Kelvin scale including absolute zero

temperature was. Thermoscopes were open at one end, were affected by air pressure, and were inaccurate. In the mid-1600s an enclosed thermometer was invented in Tuscany, Italy. This was a tube containing alcohol. It was also inaccurate. The biggest breakthrough came in 1714. Gabriel Fahrenheit (1686–1736) was a Polish craftsman and experimenter who made barometers and other instruments. He had already made an alcohol

1711 Italian naturalist Luigi Marsigli shows that corals are animals (they were previously thought to be plants).

1712 Italian mathematician Giovanni Ceva applies mathematical principles to economics.

| 1710 | 1711 | | 1712 |

1710 French chemist René-Antoine Ferchault de Réaumur creates a material woven entirely from glass fiber.

1712 English engineer Thomas Newcomen invents an atmospheric steam engine that employs a piston.

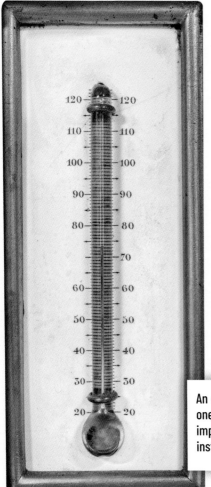

An early thermometer, one of the most important scientific instruments.

thermometer in 1709, but now he used better techniques of glassmaking to create a tube that contained the element mercury.

Fahrenheit Scale

Fahrenheit also produced a scale on his thermometer. He had fixed points for the freezing point and boiling point of water, which he called 32 degrees and 212 degrees. He then divided the length between these two points into 180 equal units. We still use this scale today.

Celsius Scale Using Fahrenheit's work as a basis, Frenchman René Réamur proposed another scale in 1731, using 80 degrees. Swedish scientist Anders Celsius (1701–1744) then devised another scale, dividing it into 100 degrees, with 0 as boiling point and 100 as freezing point. Soon after, this scale was inverted, and what we now call the Celsius scale, with 0 degrees as the freezing point of water and 100 degrees as water's boiling point, became

TIMELINE
1714–1716

KEY:

Engineering and Invention

1714 The British government offers a prize of £20,000 to the first person to devise a method of measuring longitude at sea—the prize is not claimed until 1759.

1714

1714 French physician Dominique Anel invents a fine-point syringe for medical procedures.

1714 The first typewriter is invented by English engineer Henry Mill, but no one now knows how it worked.

standard in many countries across the world.

Kelvin Scale Being able to measure temperature accurately was essential for scientific discovery. The final stage in a modern understanding of temperature came in 1848, when British scientist William Thompson, Baron Kelvin, (1824–1907) devised the Kelvin scale. This went down to what is called absolute zero, which is the temperature below which no molecules can move.

Sir William Thompson, Baron Kelvin, came up with the idea of absolute zero.

1715 The English clockmaker John Harrison invents a clock that runs for eight days on a single winding.

1716 French engineer Hubert Gautier publishes a book that is influential on bridge design.

1715

1716

1716 English astronomer Edmund Halley invents the diving bell, so that workmen can build foundations underwater.

1716 The first lighthouse is built in North America, in Boston Harbor.

Navigation at Sea

The crew of a ship at sea needs to know in what direction it is heading and its exact position. A compass shows direction, but location is far more difficult to determine.

The sextant measured a ship's position north or south of the equator.

TIMELINE
1717–1718

KEY:

Biology and Medicine

Engineering and Invention

Astronomy and Math

1717 Italian physician Giovanni Lancisi blames malaria on mosquito bites.

1717 English astronomer Abraham Sharp calculates the value of pi to 72 decimal places.

1717

1717 Death of the first Abraham Darby, who developed the process of making pig iron using coke. He has established a dynasty of ironmasters that plays a critical role in the Industrial Revolution.

Latitude indicates a position in terms of its distance north or south of the equator. It is measured in degrees. For example, Philadelphia is at a latitude of approximately 40° north. Latitude can be found by measuring the angle of a particular heavenly body above the horizon and consulting books of tables or almanacs. The angle of the polestar at night or the angle of the sun at noon can be measured and compared with tables. Early sailors had various instruments for measuring these angles. Using a cross-staff, a sailor sighted along a 3-foot- (1-m-) long staff while moving a crosspiece until the lower end lined up with the horizon and the upper end with the star or the sun. The staff was calibrated in degrees from which the sailor could read off the angle. It was first described by Levi ben Gershom (1288–1344) and used in Europe until the 18th century.

Navigators' Tools

In 1594, English sailor John Davis (c.1550–1605) invented the backstaff. This was pointed in the opposite direction to the cross-staff, meaning the operator did not need to look directly into the sun. The quadrant was a similar instrument, also used by astronomers and by gunners to set the correct angles for aiming artillery weapons.

Timeline

1594 Backstaff

1731 Octant

1735 Chronometer

1757 Sextant

1759 Harrison's prize-winning chronometer

Portolan charts appeared in the 13th century as a sailors' guide to the coast of the sea.

1718 English astronomer Edmund Halley identifies stellar proper motion, the gradual movement of stars relative to the sun.

1718 English inventor James Puckle patents a flintlock semiautomatic cannon.

1718

1718 French mathematician Abraham de Moivre writes a book on probability, *The Doctrine of Chances.*

How the Sextant Works

A navigator uses a sextant to measure the angle of the sun (or a prominent star) above the horizon. Tables convert the angle into the navigator's latitude. The index glass (in fact, a mirror) reflects the sun's rays onto the horizon glass. This half-mirror reflects the rays along a telescope to the navigator's eye. The navigator also looks through the plain (unsilvered) half of the horizon glass at the horizon and adjusts the angle of the index glass until the sun's image appears to be on the horizon. The graduated scale on the limb of the sextant then indicates the angle of the sun above the horizon.

In 1731, English mathematician John Hadley (1682–1744) invented the octant, incorrectly named Hadley's quadrant at the time. Anglo-American inventor Thomas Godfrey (1704–1749) of Philadelphia invented an almost identical instrument independently. In the octant, a pivoted arm carries a mirror that can be moved to bring an image of the sun in line with another mirror. The second mirror also gives a view of the horizon. The maximum angle it could measure was 45°. From there it was a simple step to the sextant (which

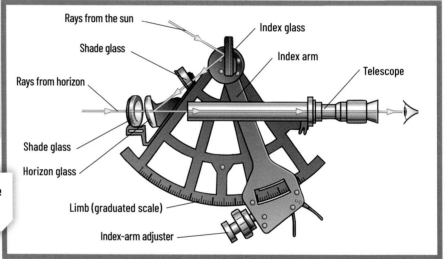

Rays from the sun
Index glass
Shade glass
Index arm
Telescope
Rays from horizon
Shade glass
Horizon glass
Limb (graduated scale)
Index-arm adjuster

This diagram shows the key parts of a sextant.

TIMELINE
1719–1724

KEY:

Biology and Medicine

Engineering and Invention

Astronomy and Math

Chemistry and Physics

1719 English mathematician Brook Taylor demonstrates the principle of the vanishing point in linear perspective.

1720 Italian harpsichord maker Bartolomeo Cristofori invents the pianoforte (piano).

1719

1720

1719 German engraver Jakob Le Blon invents a four-color printing process using blue, yellow, red, and black.

1720 English inventor Christopher Pinchbeck produces an alloy of copper and zinc; named pinchbeck, it resembles gold and is used in watches and jewelry.

measured up to 60°), introduced by Scottish naval officer John Campbell (c.1720–1790) in 1757. The sextant became the standard navigational instrument for 250 years. It was even used on aircraft until it was finally supplanted by radio beacons and the satellite-based GPS (global positioning system).

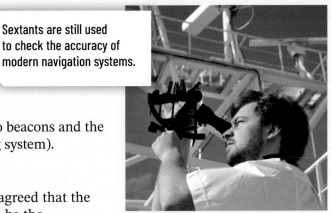

Sextants are still used to check the accuracy of modern navigation systems.

Finding Longitude

In 1884, an international conference agreed that the prime meridian (longitude 0°) should be the Greenwich meridian that runs through the Greenwich Observatory in London. The longitude of any other place is its position east or west of the Greenwich meridian. This proved to be far more difficult to work out than calculating latitude. For centuries, sailors measured the angle between the moon and another heavenly body, and consulted tables called ephemerides that gave the day-to-day positions of the moon. German

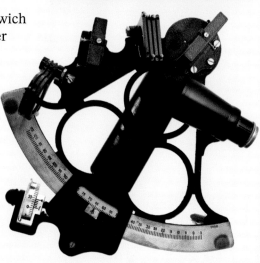

Although the design of the sextant has become more modern, the basic technology remains exactly the same as it was in 1757.

1721 American physician Zabdiel Boylston carries out the first smallpox inoculation in the United States.

1724 Dutch scientist Herman Boerhaave publishes *Elements of Chemistry*, the first major chemistry textbook.

1721

1723

1724

1723 French engineer Nicolas Bion writes a catalog of surveying instruments currently still in use.

This stone marks the prime meridian, 0° longitude, at Greenwich, England.

astronomer Johann Müller (1436–76), also known as Regiomontanus, drew up the first tables in 1474. They were published in 1766 in the *Nautical Almanac* by English astronomer Nevil Maskelyne (1732–1811) and were subsequently revised every year. The solution to the longitude problem lay in finding an accurate way of measuring time, which varies locally depending on longitude. For example, at 12:00 p.m. in London, England, it is 7:00 a.m. in Philadelphia (longitude about 75° west). So if we know the exact time at a given place when it is noon in London, its longitude can be calculated. To do this we need a chronometer, a very accurate clock. In 1714, the British government offered a prize of £20,000 to anyone who could produce such an instrument. A condition was that the "sea clock" had

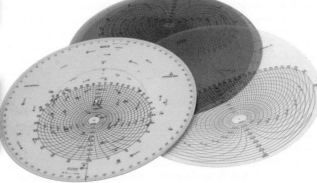

These disks were used to convert sextant readings into coordinates for navigation.

TIMELINE
1725–1727

KEY:

Biology and Medicine

Engineering and Invention

Astronomy and Math

Chemistry and Physics

1725 The Accokeek Furnace is built in Virginia to smelt iron.

1725 German physicist Johann Schulze notices that some silver salts turn dark in daylight; the discovery is significant in the development of photography.

1725

1725 French clockmaker Antoine Thiout constructs a clock that displays solar time.

1725 Scottish goldsmith William Ged invents stereotype printing, in which a mold is made of a complete page.

to gain or lose no more than 2 minutes after a six-week voyage to the West Indies and back. English clockmaker John Harrison (1693–1776) took up the challenge. In 1735, he introduced his first chronometer, but it was his fourth instrument, which he made in 1759, that won the prize (or half of it, since the government kept half the money until Harrison showed that the chronometer could be copied). He did not receive the remainder of the money until 1773, and then only after King George III pleaded Harrison's case.

Finding Longitude

Finding a ship's east-west position needs an accurate chronometer. If a ship sails from Greenwich at noon, its chronometer is set to 12 o'clock. After five days, at noon local time (gauged by sextant) the chronometer reads 4:00 p.m. The Earth has rotated on its axis for four hours since it was 12 o'clock in Greenwich. The four hours represent 4/24, or 1/6, of a complete rotation, or 1/6 of 360°, or 60°.

In this example, the ship's position is 60° west.

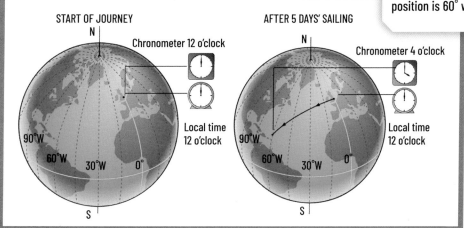

START OF JOURNEY

Chronometer 12 o'clock

Local time 12 o'clock

90°W 60°W 30°W 0°

AFTER 5 DAYS' SAILING

Chronometer 4 o'clock

Local time 12 o'clock

90°W 60°W 30°W 0°

1726 English inventor George Graham invents the mercury pendulum for clocks, which does not change length with a change in temperature.

1727 Swiss mathematician Leonhard Euler introduces the symbol "e" as the base of natural logarithms.

1726

1727

1727 English botanist Stephen Hales writes *Vegetable Staticks*, the first book on plant physiology.

Benjamin Franklin

Benjamin Franklin played an important role in the development of the United States, but he also made major discoveries in physics and was a talented inventor.

Franklin is said to have tested the electrical nature of lightning by flying a kite in a storm.

TIMELINE
1728–1730

KEY:

Biology and Medicine

Engineering and Invention

Astronomy and Math

Chemistry and Physics

1728 English clockmaker John Harrison invents the gridiron pendulum for clocks; its length is not affected by changes in temperature.

1728

1728 U.S. naturalist John Bartram opens the first botanical gardens in America, near Philadelphia.

1728 French dentist Pierre Fauchard invents the first dental drill and makes the first fillings.

Born in Boston into a family of 17 children, Benjamin Franklin left school at the age of 10. Two years later, he was apprenticed to his older brother James, a printer. When he was just 18, Benjamin took over publication of the *New England Courant*, a weekly newspaper founded by his brother. He did not stay for long; instead, he went to Philadelphia and worked as a printer himself. In 1724, he set sail for England but returned home two years later. In 1733, he published the first volume of *Poor Richard's Almanac*, a collection of articles on a wide range of subjects to "convey instruction among the common people." He held various public offices and helped draft the Declaration of Independence in 1776. He traveled to France to raise help for the American cause in the American Revolution, and in Paris witnessed the Montgolfier brothers' first hot-air balloon flight in 1783. He was a staunch supporter of the abolition of slavery; he retired from public life in 1788.

Franklin and Electricity

During his lifetime, Franklin also conducted scientific experiments. The best known, in 1752, was one of the most dangerous experiments ever

Timeline

1733 *Poor Richard's Almanac* first published

1742 Franklin stove

1752 Kite experiment and lightning rod

1784 Bifocal eyeglasses

As a politician, Franklin was one of the leading founders of the United States.

1729 English physicist Stephen Gray distinguishes between electrical insulators and conductors.

1730 French chemist René-Antoine Ferchault de Réaumur makes an alcohol thermometer.

1729

1730

1730 French surgeon George Martin performs the first tracheostomy, an operation to make a hole in the windpipe.

1730 English mathematician John Hadley devises the quadrant, an instrument for navigation at sea.

Hearth and Home

At a domestic level, Benjamin Franklin is credited with inventing the rocking chair and, in 1742, the Franklin stove, which had an underfloor draftpipe. Franklin needed eyeglasses for reading and different glasses for distance vision. Annoyed with always having to change glasses, he invented bifocals in about 1784. They had split lenses—the upper half for distance vision and the lower half for near vision. In a bid to save fuel on winter evenings, he suggested the introduction of daylight saving time.

undertaken. He attached a metal key to the moistened string of a kite, which he flew during a thunderstorm. Electric "fluid" flowing down the string caused sparks to jump between the key and a Leyden jar (a primitive electrical condenser). Franklin had established the electrical nature of lightning and he coined the words "positive" and "negative" to describe the two types of static electricity. Several European scientists who tried to repeat the experiment were struck by lightning and killed. Franklin, however, devised a means of protection. He invented

Franklin invented bifocals, which improve both near and farsighted vision.

TIMELINE
1731–1734

KEY:

Biology and Medicine

Engineering and Invention

Astronomy and Math

Chemistry and Physics

1731 English astronomer John Bevis discovers the Crab Nebula.

1731

1732

1731 English agriculturalist Jethro Tull recommends modern farming methods in a new book.

1732 French physicist Henri Pitot creates the Pitot tube, an instrument for measuring speed of airflow.

the lightning rod, a pointed conductor located at the top of a building and connected to the ground by a thick wire attached to a plate buried in the soil. Today, all tall buildings have lightning rods. He also theorized that thunderclouds are electrically charged and recognized the aurora borealis (the northern lights, visible in the sky at polar latitudes) to be electrical in nature.

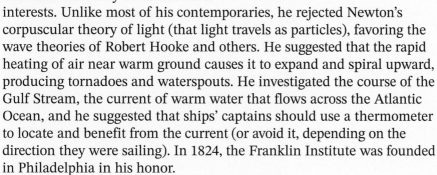

This cutaway illustration shows the flue that provided the backdraft to make the Franklin stove so highly efficient.

Other Scientific Interests

Franklin had many other scientific interests. Unlike most of his contemporaries, he rejected Newton's corpuscular theory of light (that light travels as particles), favoring the wave theories of Robert Hooke and others. He suggested that the rapid heating of air near warm ground causes it to expand and spiral upward, producing tornadoes and waterspouts. He investigated the course of the Gulf Stream, the current of warm water that flows across the Atlantic Ocean, and he suggested that ships' captains should use a thermometer to locate and benefit from the current (or avoid it, depending on the direction they were sailing). In 1824, the Franklin Institute was founded in Philadelphia in his honor.

1733 English engineer John Kay invents the flying shuttle, which speeds up the process of weaving.

1734 French chemist René-Antoine Ferchault de Réaumur writes *Memoirs Serving as a Natural History of Insects*, founding the science of entomology.

1733

1734

1733 French mathematician Abraham de Moivre discovers the normal (bell-shaped) distribution curve, which is now a major element in statistical studies.

1734 Swedish scientist Emanuel Swedenborg writes *Mineral Kingdom*, describing techniques for mining and smelting metals.

Carl Linnaeus

For thousands of years, scholars had tried to find a way of classifying life forms. Linnaeus invented a method with two names that are used in all modern taxonomy.

Listing the huge number of life forms and describing their relationship to each other was an enormous task. It had been recognized as being a problem in the fourth century BCE, when the Greek philosopher Aristotle tried to set up a system that would form a basis for the investigation of life.

One of the problems was that many species, especially species of plants, looked similar, but had different names in different countries. It was difficult to know how closely

Carl Linnaeus, the Swedish botanist who invented the system for naming species that is still used today.

TIMELINE
1735–1738

KEY:

▬▬▬
Engineering and Invention

▬▬▬
Astronomy and Math

▬▬▬
Chemistry and Physics

1735 Spanish scientist Antonio de Ulloa rediscovers platinum in South America.

1735 English physicist Stephen Gray suggests that lightning is an electrical phenomenon.

1735

1735 English clockmaker John Harrison makes a chronometer, a clock that keeps time well enough to be used to calculate longitude at sea.

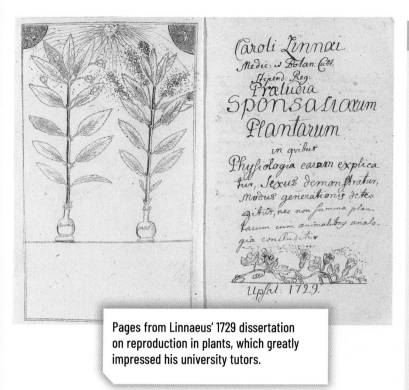

Pages from Linnaeus' 1729 dissertation on reproduction in plants, which greatly impressed his university tutors.

Timeline

c.355 BCE Greek philosopher Aristotle divides the living world into animals and plants.

1700 Joseph Pitton de Tournefort publishes his *Institutiones Rei Herbariae*, including more than 9,000 plant species

1734 French chemist René-Antoine Ferchault de Réaumur founds the science of entomology

1735 Swedish naturalist Carolus Linnaeus (1707–1778) publishes *Systema Naturae*, classifying objects into three kingdoms: animal, plant, and mineral

1813 The term "taxonomy" is introduced by Auguste Pyramus de Candolle

related these plants were to each other. It was also difficult to decide on what name should be applied to a species when it was known worldwide by different names in different languages. Scholars tried to solve this problem as they carried out more detailed research.

1737 Swedish chemist Georg Brandt discovers cobalt, the first completely new metal discovered since ancient times.

1738 Swiss scientist Daniel Bernoulli suggests that the behavior of gases is explained if they are made up of tiny particles of matter.

1736 **1537** **1738**

1736 French surveyor Alexis Clairaut measures the length of 1 degree of meridian (longitude), allowing accurate calculation of the size of Earth.

1738 English metallurgist William Champion devises a new industrial process for the extraction of zinc from its ores.

1738 English inventor Lewis Paul produces a machine for carding wool, or combing it into parallel fibers.

A solution was finally devised by Swedish botanist Carl Linnaeus (1707–1778). He adopted the name Linnaeus after the Swedish word for lime tree.

Classification System

Linnaeus was interested in plants from an early age. He studied at Uppsala University, where he was giving lectures to fellow students long before he had graduated. In 1732, he made an expedition to the little-known northern area of Lapland, studying plants and the Sami people who lived there. His published description of the plants he found there (*Flora Lapponica*) used his new system of classification. This system was simple. Each species was given a first name that fitted it

Linnaeus in the Sami clothes he wore while exploring in Lapland.

TIMELINE
1740–1743

KEY:

Biology and Medicine

Engineering and Invention

Astronomy and Math

Chemistry and Physics

1740 Swiss naturalist Charles Bonnet observes parthenogenesis in aphids, in which unfertilized females give birth.

1742 American scientist and politician Benjamin Franklin invents a wood-burning stove.

1740

1742

1740 English metallurgist Benjamin Huntsman invents the crucible process for making steel in batches.

1742 Swedish astronomer Anders Celsius introduces the 100-degree Celsius (or centigrade) temperature scale.

into a higher class, and a specific second name that identified the species. He proposed three broad groups, or kingdoms—animals, plants, and minerals—and divided each of these kingdoms into classes.

Linnaeus' classification system became universally employed partly because he was very good at tracing the relationship between species and the higher classes to which they belonged. At the same time, names could be easily changed if mistakes were made. The Linnaean system also used Latin words, and this was the international scholarly language within Europe at the time. This made the classification of species useful to all botanists.

CAROLI LINNÆI
EQUITIS DE STELLA POLARI,
ARCHIATRI REGII, MED. & BOTAN. PROFESS. UPSAL.;
ACAD. UPSAL. HOLMENS. PETROPOL. BEROL. IMPER.
LOND. MONSPEL. TOLOS. FLORENT. SOC.

SYSTEMA NATURÆ
PER
REGNA TRIA NATURÆ,
SECUNDUM
CLASSES, ORDINES,
GENERA, SPECIES,
CUM
*CHARACTERIBUS, DIFFERENTIIS,
SYNONYMIS, LOCIS.*

TOMUS I.

EDITIO DECIMA, REFORMATA.

Cum Privilegio S:æ R:æ M:tis Sveciæ.

HOLMIÆ,
IMPENSIS DIRECT. LAURENTII SALVII,
1758.

The frontispiece of Linnaeus' most important work, the *Systema Naturae*, which went through many new editions during the mid 1700s.

1743 The American Philosophical Society is founded.

1743 English metalworker Thomas Boulsover produces "Sheffield plate," metalware consisting of copper coated with a thin layer of silver.

1743

1743 English mathematician Thomas Simpson devises a systematic approach to finding the area bounded by a curve.

The Steam Engine

People relied on wind, water, or animal power for energy until the invention of the steam engine, which culminated in 1765 with the work of James Watt.

Mines used steam engines to run pumps that removed water from underground.

TIMELINE
1745–1747

KEY:

Biology and Medicine

Chemistry and Physics

1745 French surgeon Jacques Daviel successfully performs an operation for the removal of a cataract from a patient's eye.

1745

1745 Russian scientist Mikhail Lomonosov compiles a catalog of more than 300 minerals.

1745 Dutch physicist Pieter van Musschenbroek invents the Leyden jar, a simple form of electrical condenser.

The earliest steam engines are more accurately called atmospheric engines; they used the pressure of the air. The first was devised by French physicist Denis Papin. A vertical, open-ended cylinder with a close-fitting piston had water inside its base. A fire heated the base of the cylinder, causing the water to boil and turn into steam. Steam pressure lifted the piston, which remained raised while the cylinder cooled. The steam condensed back to liquid water, creating a partial vacuum in the cylinder. Then atmospheric pressure on the upper end of the piston pushed it down again. A rope connected to the piston and moving over a pulley could be used to lift a load or work a pump.

Savery's Steam Pump

A similar arrangement, patented in 1698 by English mining engineer Thomas Savery, made the atmospheric engine into a practical steam pump. It had no piston or other moving parts, just hand-operated valves to provide continuous operation. Steam from a boiler passed into a working chamber that was sprayed with cold water to condense the steam. The partial vacuum that was created as a result lifted water through a one-way valve into the chamber. Steam was then let in again, which forced the water out and up

Timeline

1690 Papin's primitive engine

1698 Savery's atmospheric steam pump

1712 Newcomen's atmospheric steam engine

1765 Watt's engine with external condenser

1801 Trevithick's double-action, high-pressure engine

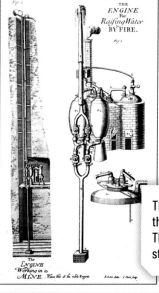

This diagram shows the workings of Thomas Savery's steam pump of 1698.

1747 German chemist Andreas Marggraf recognizes that there are sugars in agricultural beets.

1747 French monk Jean-Antoine Nollet devises an electrometer (an instrument for measuring electrical charge).

1746

1747

1746 English chemist John Roebuck develops the lead-chamber process for making sulfuric acid.

1747 Scottish physician James Lind experiments with citrus fruits to prevent scurvy among sailors in the British Royal Navy.

Newcomen's Steam Engine

In Newcomen's engine, steam from a boiler forced a piston up an open-ended cylinder; cold water sprayed into the cylinder condensed the steam, creating a partial vacuum that sucked the piston down again. The piston joined to one end of a long beam; the other end of the beam connected to a pump. As the piston went up and down, the beam rocked and worked the pump up and down in a continuous motion.

through another one-way valve.
In 1712, English engineer Thomas Newcomen perfected the first engine to use steam pressure to work a piston. They were

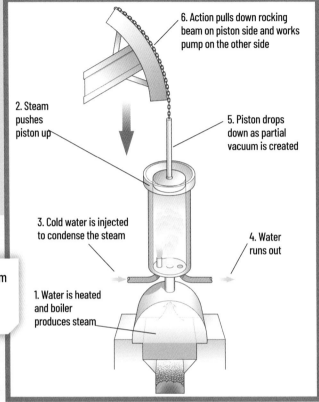

6. Action pulls down rocking beam on piston side and works pump on the other side

2. Steam pushes piston up

5. Piston drops down as partial vacuum is created

3. Cold water is injected to condense the steam

4. Water runs out

1. Water is heated and boiler produces steam

Newcomen's engine used steam to push the piston directly, unlike atmospheric engines.

TIMELINE
1748–1750

KEY:

Biology and Medicine

Engineering and Invention

Astronomy and Math

1748 Scottish physician John Fothergill gives the first description of diphtheria.

1748

1748 English astronomer James Bradley discovers the nutation of Earth, or the slight nodding of Earth's axis as it orbits.

usually called beam engines. Newcomen could not patent his engine because its principle was too close to that of Thomas Savery's, so instead the two men went into partnership. In 1764, Scottish engineer James Watt received a model of a Newcomen engine to repair. He realized how much energy is wasted by first heating the cylinder and then cooling it. In 1765, Watt added a separate external condenser. In addition, he used steam to push the piston up and then—by admitting low-pressure steam on the other side—to push it down in a double action.

Trevithick's Engines

In 1800, Watt's master patent expired. The following year, English inventor Richard Trevithick started to build double-action, high-pressure engines. Trevithick removed the separate condenser and used the waste steam to preheat the water entering the boiler. Within four years, he built nearly 50 engines that were used mainly in mines in Britain and eventually in countries in South America.

Richard Trevithick developed the highly efficient double-action, high-pressure engine.

By their very action, early steam engines produced an up-and-down motion. But most machines of the time, except pumps, required rotary motion. Until the advent of the steam engine, most of them had been driven by waterwheels. Then, in 1781, James Watt had invented the sun-and-planet gear to make his engines provide a rotary final drive.

1749 Carolus Linnaeus introduces binomial naming for animals and plants, using genus and species names.

1750 German engineer Johann Segner constructs a waterwheel in which the wheel is turned by the force of a jet of water.

1749

1750

1750 French astronomer Guillaume Le Gentil de la Galasière discovers the Trifid Nebula in the constellation Sagittarius.

James Watt

One of history's greatest engineers, James Watt produced the first reliable engines to power textile mills and pump water out of mines.

The key to Watt's engine was the condenser (the small cylinder at left).

TIMELINE
1751–1755

KEY:

Biology and Medicine

Engineering and Invention

Astronomy and Math

Chemistry and Physics

1751 French astronomer Nicolas de Lacaille makes observations that allow the first accurate calculations of the distance from Earth to the moon.

1751

1751 In France, Denis Diderot is about to publish his *Encyclopedia*, an attempt to gather together all useful knowledge in one great multi-volume work.

1751 Swedish chemist Axel Cronstedt discovers nickel.

In legend, Watt was inspired to make a steam engine by watching a kettle boil.

Timeline

1765 Steam engine with separate condenser

1769 Watt patents his steam engine

1775 Partnership with Matthew Boulton

1781 Sun-and-planet gear

1782 Double-acting steam engine

1788 Flying-ball governor

Scottish engineer James Watt (1736–1819) learned technical skills from his father, a carpenter. In 1755, Watt worked in London as an apprentice to a maker of mathematical instruments. Two years later, he was appointed instrument maker at Glasgow University and had his own workshop.

Improving the Steam Engine

The university had a model of a Newcomen steam engine, and in 1764 Watt was asked to repair it. He realized that the alternate heating and cooling processes of the cylinder wasted a lot of energy. It was heated by steam and then cooled by cold water sprayed into the cylinder to condense the steam.

In 1765, Watt made an engine that overcame the difficulty by leading the steam into a separate condenser so that the cylinder could remain hot all

James Watt performs an experiment in his workshop.

1752 American scientist and politician Benjamin Franklin demonstrates the electrical nature of lightning in a famous kite-flying experiment.

1753 Scottish engineer Charles Morrison invents a 26-wire telegraph (one wire for each letter of the alphabet).

1752

1753

1755

1752 French chemist René-Antoine Ferchault de Réaumur discovers how gastric juices operate in digestion.

1755 German philosopher Immanuel Kant proposes a theory that the solar system was created from a spinning gaseous nebula and that our galaxy is just one of many in the universe.

James Watt is remembered in the SI unit of power, the watt, which was named in his honor.

Watt invented a machine for copying ancient busts, like this portrait of Aristotle.

the time, making the engine three times more efficient. Watt moved from Scotland to England, and in 1775 went into business with Matthew Boulton to manufacture Watt's engine, which he had patented in 1769. The first machine of 1776 needed five years of development before it was reliable enough for quantity production, and Watt constantly fought legal battles over infringement of his patent. Most of the engines he made were used as pumps to replace the 50-year-old Newcomen engines in tin and copper mines.

Improvements

Watt worked to improve his engine. In order to convert the up-and-down motion of the piston into rotary motion, he invented the sun-and-planet gear and the connecting rod-and-crank system in 1781. The innovations made the engine useful for driving lathes, looms, and cranes. In 1782, Watt produced a double-acting steam engine in which steam is let in alternately on each side of the piston. The machine used steam power on every stroke. He devised the flying-ball centrifugal governor in 1788 to control an engine's speed. His invention of the pressure gauge in 1790 completed his

TIMELINE
1756–1758

KEY:

Engineering and Invention

Astronomy and Math

Chemistry and Physics

1756 English engineer John Smeaton invents "hydraulic lime," cement that hardens underwater.

1757 English engineer Henry Berry builds the Sankey Brook Navigation, the first modern canal.

1756

1757

1757 English clockmaker Thomas Mudge invents a lever escapement for a watch, which is first used in 1770.

engine, and by the end of the 18th century there were nearly 500 Watt steam engines in use. Their output was measured in horsepower, which was another of James Watt's innovations.

Watt's other achievements included a method of copying documents using a special ink. This hectograph was patented in 1780. Another of his inventions was a sculpting machine for reproducing busts and figures. In 1794, he became a founder of the new company of Boulton, Watt and Sons. Watt retired in 1800 and lived to see his son, James Watt Jr., receive acclaim in 1817 for making the engines for the *Caledonia*, the first seagoing steamship to be launched from an English port.

The Centrifugal Governor

James Watt devised the governor to control his steam engines. A belt (1), driven by the engine, rotates a vertical shaft on the governor. As it turns, it flings the weights (2) outward by centrifugal force. As they go around, they rise (3), lifting the rod (4). The rod works a valve that controls the supply of steam to the engine. Reducing the steam supply slows the engine; but as it slows, the rod gradually falls and lets in more steam. The device is an example of feedback control.

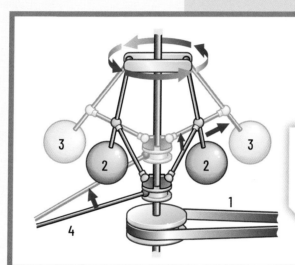

Watt's centrifugal governor made sure that an engine did not operate too fast.

1758 Halley's comet returns, as was predicted by Edmund Halley in 1682.

1758 English weaver Jedediah Strutt invents the stocking frame, for making hosiery.

1758

1758 French astronomer Charles Messier rediscovers the Crab Nebula and designates it M1 in his catalog of nebulas.

1758 German chemist Andreas Marggraf introduces flame tests as part of chemical analysis (various elements burn different colors).

Textiles

Textile machinery was at the forefront of the Industrial Revolution. Within just 70 years, the Western textile industry became totally mechanized.

The loom lifts warp threads to allow weft threads to pass between them.

TIMELINE
1760–1763

KEY:

Biology and Medicine

Engineering and Invention

Astronomy and Math

Chemistry and Physics

1760 Swiss physicist Johann Lambert formulates Lambert's law, about the angle and brightness of reflected light.

1761 English engineer James Brindley completes the construction of the Bridgewater Canal near Manchester, England.

1760

1761

1761 Russian scientist Mikhail Lomonosov observes a transit of Venus across the sun and deduces that Venus has an atmosphere.

1761 Scottish chemist Joseph Black describes how "latent heat" is needed to make a substance either melt or boil.

Cotton fibers, like those of wool, need to be twisted into yarn before they can be used.

Timeline

1200s Spinning wheel

1733 Flying shuttle

1764 Spinning jenny

1769 Spinning frame

1779 Spinning mule

1785 Steam-powered loom

The development of the mechanical spinning mule—which was the key to the mechanization of the textile industry—from the hand-operated spinning wheel took more than 600 years. After that, mechanization was rapid.

The first aid to spinning was the distaff, which consists of a long stick onto which wool is loosely wound. The spinner (or spinster), in most cultures usually a woman, held the distaff under her arm and teased out a continuous strand of wool, which she spun between the fingers of the other hand. The spun thread wound itself around a rotating spindle at the end of the distaff. Historians have learned that the ancient Mesopotamians used the distaff 7,500 years ago, and it competes with the wheel as one of the oldest-known inventions.

This spinning wheel has a foot treadle, so that the spinster can work sitting down.

1761 Italian physician Giovanni Morgagni founds the science of pathology, or understanding disease.

1761

1762

1763

1762 In France, the world's first national veterinarian college opens.

1763 German botanist Josef Kölreuter discovers the role of insects in the pollination of flowers.

The Loom

A loom consists of a frame to hold sets of parallel warp threads. The weft (crosswise) thread is wound on a shuttle, which the weaver works in and out of the lengthwise threads. Another frame, the heddle, holds vertical wires ending in rings through which the warp threads move. Controlled by treadles, the heddle lifts various sets of warp threads to create different kinds of weave.

The spinning jenny allowed a worker to spin many strands of yarn simultaneously. The machine was invented by English mechanic James Hargreaves in 1764.

Making Yarn

The spinning wheel, which was in regular use in Europe from the 1200s, simplified the task by using a large vertical wheel to wind the yarn. It had a belt drive to spin the spindle, while the spinner pulled a strand of wool from a vertical distaff. With her other hand she turned the wheel, although this task was mechanized by the addition of a foot treadle in the 16th century. The rocking motion of the treadle turned the upright wheel.

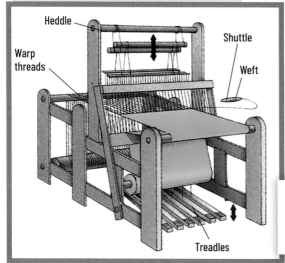

Heddle
Shuttle
Warp threads
Weft
Treadles

This diagram shows the parts of a loom; the finished cloth is wound in a roll underneath.

TIMELINE
1764–1765

KEY:

Biology and Medicine

Engineering and Invention

Astronomy and Math

1764

1764 English mechanic James Hargreaves invents the spinning jenny for spinning many threads of cotton or wool at the same time. It is a key step in the Industrial Revolution.

1764 French engineer Pierre Trésaguet introduces a new system of road building in France.

1764 Italian-born French mathematician Joseph Lagrange explains why the motion of the moon allows us to see more than 50 percent of its surface.

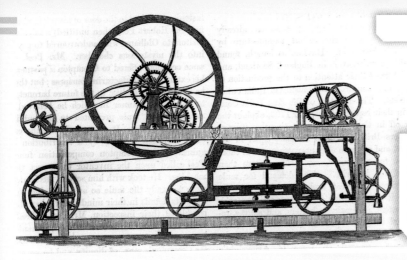

Samuel Crompton's spinning mule allowed one spinster to produce 48 strands of fine yarn at the same time.

Two major advances came in the 18th century during the earliest stages of the Industrial Revolution. The English mechanic James Hargreaves (c.1720–1778) invented the spinning jenny in 1764 (he patented his device in 1770), and the spinning frame was invented by his compatriot Richard Arkwright (1732–1792) in 1769. The spinning jenny was originally turned by hand and was mostly used to produce woolen yarn (eight threads at once on the first machines). The spinning frame was powered by a waterwheel (early cotton and woolen mills usually stood on streams for that reason) and made cotton yarn strong enough to act as the warp (lengthwise) threads in weaving.

The two ideas—the jenny and the spinning frame—were brought together in 1779 by the English weaver Samuel Crompton (1753–1827), who invented a device that became known as the spinning mule. It produced 48 strands of fine yarn at the same time. It is said to have been named "mule" because it is a hybrid of the two earlier machines.

1765 The world's first mining academy is opened in Freiberg, Germany.

1765 American scientist John Winthrop attempts to calculate the masses of comets.

1765

1765 Italian researcher Lazzaro Spallanzi preserves food by putting it in an hermetically sealed (airtight) container.

1765 Scottish engineer James Watt builds a steam engine with a separate condenser.

Just a handful of workers look after a mill full of self-acting cotton mules.

Rovings into Threads

In principle, roving machines are similar in their operation. The textile fibers, known as rovings, are wound onto rotating spindles that move on a frame. The frame first pulls the strands outward, twisting them to form yarn; it then moves back while the yarn is wound onto bobbins. After 1828, cotton was usually spun on the ring-spinning frame invented by the American John Thorpe. The rovings go through a set of high-speed rollers that draw them into fine threads. Each thread then moves through a hole in a "traveler," which twists the thread as it winds it onto a rapidly rotating vertical bobbin.

Mechanizing Weaving

Having produced the yarn, the weaver then has to make it into cloth by weaving the threads together. This is the function of the loom. At its simplest, the loom is a frame that holds a set of parallel threads called the warp. The weaver interweaves them at right angles with another thread—known as the weft—that is carried on a bobbin in a boat-shaped holder known as a shuttle. The first improvement was the addition of cords that pulled up every other warp thread to make it easier to pass the shuttle from side to side. Soon weavers added treadles to work the cords.

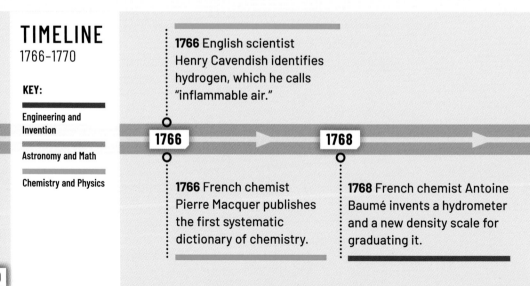

TIMELINE
1766–1770

KEY:

Engineering and Invention

Astronomy and Math

Chemistry and Physics

1766 English scientist Henry Cavendish identifies hydrogen, which he calls "inflammable air."

1766

1768

1766 French chemist Pierre Macquer publishes the first systematic dictionary of chemistry.

1768 French chemist Antoine Baumé invents a hydrometer and a new density scale for graduating it.

The process of weaving sped up greatly in 1733 when the English engineer John Kay (1704–c.1780) invented the so-called flying shuttle, a mechanism that enables the weaver to "throw" the shuttle rapidly from side to side of the loom through the warp threads. Mechanized looms came next, driven by waterpower at first, then by steam engines after 1785, the year that English inventor Edmund Cartwright (1743–1823) created the first steam-powered loom.

Different Patterns of Weaves

A loom produces different kinds of weave depending on the combination of warp threads lifted by the heddle. Shown here are sateen weave (1), satin weave (2), twill weave (3), and plain weave (4).

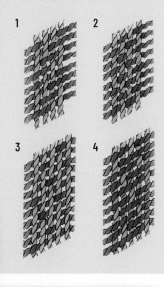

Children walk to work at a mill. Children were used to look after the machines.

1769 English manufacturer Richard Arkwright produces the spinning frame for spinning strong cotton thread.

1769 English explorer James Cook leads an expedition to Tahiti to observe a transit of Venus across the sun.

1769

1770

1769 English chemist Joseph Priestly formulates his first laws about the nature of electrical forces.

1770 English chemist Joseph Priestly invents the pencil eraser.

Antoine Lavoisier

In the late 1700s, many researchers were trying to find out what happens when a substance burns. Antoine Lavoisier provided the answer. He is known as the father of modern chemistry.

Born in 1743 as the aristocrat Antoine-Laurent de Lavoisier, Lavoisier used the wealth he made from collecting taxes for the French monarchy to fund his chemical research and help other researchers.

Phlogiston

From about 1670, many researchers had believed in a theory that when something burns (or when iron rusts), a substance called phlogiston is

A portrait of Lavoisier and his wife, Marie-Anne Paulze Lavoisier, who was also a remarkable chemist.

TIMELINE
1770–1772

KEY:

Biology and Medicine

Engineering and Invention

Astronomy and Math

Chemistry and Physics

1770

1770 French watchmaker Abraham-Louis Perrelet develops a watch with automatic winding.

1771 Italian physician Luigi Galvini shows that the muscles of a dissected frog twitch when they are stimulated by electricity.

1771

1771 Jean Deluc discovers how to use a barometer to find the height of mountains, realizing that pressure decreases as he goes higher.

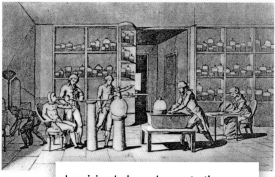

Lavoisier during a demonstration in the 1770s. His experiments led to a revolution in chemistry.

Timeline

1766 English scientist Henry Cavendish identifies hydrogen, which he describes as "inflammable air"

1772 Scottish chemist Daniel Rutherford discovers nitrogen

1772 Swedish chemist Karl Scheele discovers oxygen but does not publish his findings until 1777

1774 English chemist Joseph Priestley identifies oxygen and publishes his findings

1774 French chemist Antoine Lavoisier demonstrates the law of conservation

released into the air. This explained why most things that burned seemed to become lighter. The ash in a wood fire, for example, was much lighter than the wood before it was burned. Some scientists realized this could not be the entire solution, because they could see that when some metals burned, the result was something heavier.

Gases such as hydrogen, nitrogen, and oxygen were being discovered and experimented on during the 1770s. Lavoisier carried out his experiments in a "closed environment," from which no air could escape, and showed that rather than losing mass, when phosphorus

1772 French mineralogist Jean Romé de l'Isle argues that crystals have constant angles between their faces.

1772 Swedish chemist Karl Scheele discovers oxygen but does not publish his findings until 1777.

1772

1772 Rice has been introduced and is being grown and exported from what is now the Carolinas and Georgia.

1772 Scottish chemist Daniel Rutherford discovers nitrogen.

English scientist Joseph Priestley often corresponded with Lavoisier, but was unwilling to abandon his phlogiston theory when Lavoisier first proved him to be wrong.

burned it reacted with something in the air and the weight of the burnt material increased. He realized that something in the air was reacting with the phosphorus. This substance was oxygen. Lavoisier then realized that rather than matter increasing or decreasing during the burning process, the amount of matter actually stayed the same but the burning process changed the nature of the substances because they were reacting with oxygen. This discovery is called the law of conservation.

Making Distinctions

Lavoisier went on from this radical discovery to assemble a list of basic substances from which all others could be made. This list is no longer used, but his system of describing compounds, such as showing the differences between sulfuric acid and

TIMELINE
1773–1774

KEY:

Engineering and Invention

Astronomy and Math

Chemistry and Physics

1773 German-born English astronomer William Herschel figures out that the sun is gradually moving through space.

1774 In Sweden, Karl Scheele identifies barium, chlorine, and manganese.

1773

1774

1774 In Germany, Johann Bode publishes the first *Astronomisches Jahrbuch* (Astronomical Yearbook).

sulfurous acid are still of use. Lavoisier's ability to make such fine distinctions was important for the future development of chemistry.

Lavoisier was on the side of reform during the French Revolution from 1789. He helped to create the metric system of weights and measures, for example. But his role in collecting taxes for the discredited monarchy led to his being killed by guillotine in 1794.

Street violence during the French Revolution. Lavoisier sympathized with the revolutionaries, but was wrongly found guilty of corruption and beheaded in 1794.

1774 English astronomer Nevil Maskelyne calculates the average density of Earth.

1774 French chemist Antoine Lavoisier demonstrates the law of the conservation of mass in a chemical reaction.

1774

1774 English chemist Joseph Priestley identifies oxygen and publishes his findings.

1774 English engineer John Wilkinson patents a cannon-boring machine.

Farm Machinery

Farming technology was generally ancient until cast-iron plowshares appeared in Europe and the United States toward the end of the 18th century.

This combine thresher was pulled by 30 horses and needed four people to operate it.

TIMELINE
1775–1777

KEY:

Biology and Medicine

Engineering and Invention

Astronomy and Math

Chemistry and Physics

1775 German geologist Abraham Werner proposes—wrongly—the theory that the rocks in Earth's crust were created by the action of water.

1775

1776

1775 Danish naturalist Johann Fabricius develops a classification system for insects.

1776 Uric acid is discovered by Swedish chemist Karl Scheele.

Cast-iron plowshares were invented in England and the United States in the 1780s and 1790s. Pulled by horses, they could cut through the soil deeper than wooden plows. A plow made completely of cast iron was invented in 1819 and produced in quantity in 1839 by the American industrialist John Deere. By 1862, Dutch farmers were using steam traction engines to winch plowshares in wheeled frames back and forth across a field. Other farmers used steam tractors to pull standard plows.

Stages of the Harvest

The planting of seeds became mechanized by the invention of the seed drill in 1701. After harvesting, crops such as wheat had to be threshed to remove the grain; this was mechanized by the threshing machine in 1786. The last major farming process to be mechanized was reaping. Credit usually goes to U.S. engineer Cyrus McCormick, who patented a reaper in 1834 and soon produced them on a large scale. In 1879, he created the McCormick Harvesting Machine Company, which owned a factory in

Timeline

1701 Mechanical seed drill

1785 Cast-iron plowshare

1786 Threshing machine

1819 Cast-iron plow

1834 Reaping machine

1838 Combine harvester

1878 Binding machine

1908 Steam caterpillar tractor

1935 All-crop harvester

This scene from the late 1700s shows a plow, a roller, a harrow, and a seed drill.

1776 John Fothergill, a Scottish doctor, realizes that trigeminal neuralgia (nerve pain in the face) is a disease that can be treated.

1776 American inventor David Bushnell builds the *Turtle*, one of the first submarines.

1776

1777

1776 English chemist Joseph Priestley synthesizes "laughing gas"—nitrous oxide, used as an anesthetic by dentists.

1777 French physicist Charles Coulomb invents the torsion balance, a sensitive device for measuring forces.

Jethro Tull's Seed Drill

The mechanical seed drill was invented in 1701 by English agriculturist Jethro Tull (1674–1741). Using this machine, the farmer could sow the seed in parallel rows, making the crop easier to weed by hoeing, and also easier to harvest.

An image of back-breaking farm work before the Industrial Revolution changed agricultural methods.

This early 20th-century seed drill worked in the same way as Tull's original.

Chicago that made 4,000 machines a year. In 1827, Scottish clergyman Patrick Bell had invented a reaper and sent four examples to the United States. In 1833, U.S. engineer Obed Hussey invented yet another type of reaper. His improved machine of 1847 was better than McCormick's for reaping grass and making hay, but Hussey did not have McCormick's business sense.

TIMELINE
1778–1779

KEY:

Biology and Medicine

Engineering and Invention

Chemistry and Physics

1778 German-born physician Friedrich Mesmer practices a form of hypnotism known as mesmerism (he is later denounced as a fraud).

1778

1778 English inventor Joseph Bramah patents a flushing toilet.

1778 Methane is discovered by Alexander Volta, who will later become famous for his researches into electricity.

This reaper and binder was invented and widely marketed by Cyrus McCormick.

Combine Harvesters

In the 1830s, after pioneering work by U.S. blacksmith John Lane, engineers began to make combine harvesters that cut the wheat and then bundled it into sheaves. Separate binding machines were invented later, notably by John Appleby in 1878. Later combines also threshed the grain, but the machines needed 10 or more horses to pull them.
The invention of the steam traction engine and, in 1908, the steam caterpillar tractor, overcame this disadvantage. Two years later, gasoline-driven combine harvesters began to take over. At first, a separate tractor pulled the harvester; later designers incorporated the motive power as part of the harvesting machine, and ranks of self-propelled combines became a common sight on the prairies.

1779 Dutch-born British scientist Ian Ingenhousz describes the process of photosynthesis in plants.

1779 Swiss scientist Horace de Saussure coins the term "geology" for the study of the origin and structure of Earth.

1779

1779 English weaver Samuel Crompton builds the spinning mule, which twists fibers into yarns and winds them onto bobbins.

Canals

The main way of moving heavy goods across the country in the late 18th century was by canal. Raw materials and finished goods were transported by barges towed by horses.

The Bridgewater Canal in northern England was the first modern canal.

TIMELINE
1780–1782

KEY:

Biology and Medicine

Engineering and Invention

Astronomy and Math

Chemistry and Physics

1780 Italian naturalist Lazzaro Spallanzani carries out artificial insemination on dogs.

1780

1780 American physician Benjamin Rush describes dengue fever.

Chinese engineers built the first canals for transportation more than 2,000 years ago. Extensive canal systems were used for drainage and irrigation in northern India, and by the Middle Ages they were being used in the Netherlands. Canals for industrial transportation were first used in England in 1757 after the engineer Henry Berry (1720–1812) completed the Sankey Brook Navigation near St. Helens in northern England. The canal at St. Helens included a pair of side-by-side locks known as staircase locks.

Timeline

1757 Sankey Brook Navigation

1761 Bridgewater Canal

1779 Coteau-du-Lac Canal

1825 Erie Canal

The First Canals

The first canal of importance was the Bridgewater Canal near Manchester, England. It was designed by engineer James Brindley (1716–1772) and completed in 1761. At its narrowest, it was 26 feet (8 m) wide, and was a contour (gravity-flow) canal with no locks. A canal that takes a more direct route needs locks for coping with inclines, tunnels for going through hills, and aqueducts for crossing valleys.

On Brindley's later canals, the locks were just over 13 feet (4 m) wide. For this reason, the barges that sailed on these canals had to be narrower than that, but they could be up to 72 feet (22 m) long,

The Bridgewater Canal crossed the Irwell River on a stone viaduct.

1781 French astronomer Charles Messier publishes his Messier catalog of nebulas and galaxies.

1782 Scottish engineer James Watt invents a double-acting steam engine in which steam is admitted to each side of the piston alternately.

1781

1782

1781 French mineralogist René Haüy suggests that crystals contain "unit cells," leading to his theory of crystal structure.

The Erie Canal between the Great Lakes and the Hudson River opened in 1825.

the maximum length of a lock. These boats were called narrowboats. They could carry a load of 33 tons (30 metric tons), while a wagon could carry just 2.2 tons (2 metric tons) and a packhorse's load could not usually exceed about 300 pounds (136 kg).

Other canals soon followed. In 1773, the British government commissioned Scottish engineer James Watt (1736–1819) to survey a route in Scotland that would link a series of lochs (freshwater lakes) in order to join the North Sea and the North Atlantic Ocean. Site engineer Thomas Telford (1757–1834), a fellow Scot, began work in 1803, and the first vessel sailed through the canal in 1822. The first canal to take seagoing ships was completed in England in 1819 to connect the southwest town of Exeter with the sea.

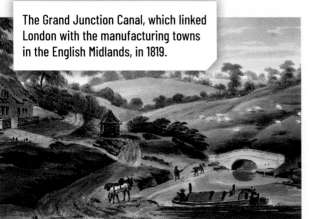

The Grand Junction Canal, which linked London with the manufacturing towns in the English Midlands, in 1819.

Canals in North America

In North America, the first canal with locks was probably the short waterway at Coteau-du-Lac, Quebec, built in 1779 by English engineer William Twiss (1745–1827) to bypass a stretch of rough water on the St. Lawrence River. In 1825, the Erie Canal was completed to carry grain from the Great Lakes region to

TIMELINE
1783-1784

KEY:

Engineering and Invention

Astronomy and Math

Chemistry and Physics

1783 Francois-Pierre Argand, a Swiss scientist, invents the Argand oil lamp. This uses air to make the flame up to 10 times brighter than previous lamps.

1783 French brothers Joseph and Jacques Montgolfier invent the hot-air balloon.

1783

1783 English physicist John Michell predicts the existence of "dark stars," now called black holes.

New York City via the Hudson River. The 362-mile (583-km) canal was 39 feet (12 m) wide and 4 feet (1.2 m) deep and needed 83 locks to cross the high ground west of Troy. In less than 10 years, receipts from tolls more than repaid the $7 million spent on its construction. The enlarged modern canal, which is now part of the New York State canal system, can carry barges of up to 2,204 tons (2,000 metric tons).

How a Pound Lock Works

A canal lock has a pair of hinged gates at each end, and sluices that can be raised or lowered to let water in and out of the lock. If a boat approaches from upstream, the sluices in the upstream gates are opened until the lock is full of water.

1. The gates open to allow the boat to enter the lock.

2. The gates close and the sluices in the lower gates open until the water level falls to match the level downstream.

3. The gates are opened to allow the boat to exit the lock.

The pound, or chamber, lock allows canals to rise and fall with the land.

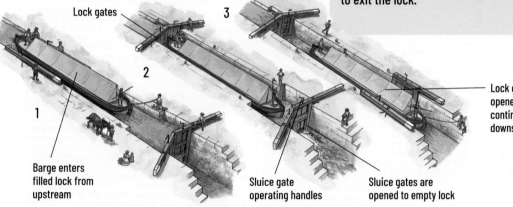

Lock gates

3

2

1

Lock gate is opened, barge continues downstream

Barge enters filled lock from upstream

Sluice gate operating handles

Sluice gates are opened to empty lock

1784 American scientist and politician Benjamin Franklin invents bifocal eyeglasses.

1784 English scientist Henry Cavendish proves that water is a compound of oxygen and hydrogen, rather than an element.

1784

1784 French chemist Antoine Lavoisier shows that matter is indestructible, and develops a theory of the conservation of mass.

Edward Jenner

In the 1700s, smallpox was a deadly disease that killed many thousands of people every year. Edward Jenner found an effective way to protect against the disease.

Smallpox was once a most deadly disease. Victims would be covered in pus-filled blisters. If patients were not killed by the disease, it was likely to leave them pockmarked and blind. Smallpox is estimated to have killed over 250,000 people per year in Europe during the 1700s.

However, a method of preventing smallpox was discovered in China. This was to give a healthy person a small dose of smallpox, using a dried scab from a blister or a small amount of pus, which was then rubbed into a scratch in the skin. The patient would usually develop a mild form of smallpox, and be immune to the disease afterward.

Edward Jenner, doctor and scientist, who introduced a method of vaccination to give people immunity from smallpox.

TIMELINE
1785–1788

KEY:

Biology and Medicine

Engineering and Invention

Astronomy and Math

1785 English inventor Edmund Cartwright makes a steam-powered loom.

1785 English engineer Robert Ransome invents the cast-iron plowshare.

1785

1785 English physician William Withering introduces the drug digitalis, made from the foxglove plant, to treat heart disorders.

British aristocrat Lady Mary Montagu saw this treatment being used in Turkey. When she returned to England she used it on her children and urged others to do the same. At about the same time in Boston, part of the colony of Massachusetts, a program of inoculation was carried out in 1721. The problem with this variolation, as the process was called, was that some patients who were given smallpox developed a full-blown version of the disease and died or were blinded. The treatment was not well received.

Lady Mary Montagu saw the process of variolation being used in Turkey and tried to introduce it to Britain.

Timeline

1500 BCE The earliest evidence of smallpox, found in Egyptian mummies

1717 English aristocrat Lady Mary Montagu describes in a letter how inoculation is carried out in Turkey, part of the Ottoman Empire, using a small amount of pus from a smallpox victim

1721 American physician Zabdiel Boylston carries out the first smallpox inoculation in the United States

1796 Edward Jenner introduces the modern smallpox vaccine, using cowpox to give immunity

1980 The World Health Organization announces that smallpox has been eradicated

1787 German-born English astronomer William Herschel observes Oberon and Titania, two moons of the planet Uranus (which he discovered in 1781).

1788 French mathematician Joseph Lagrange publishes a book analyzing the calculus of mechanics.

1786 — 1787 — 1788

1786 German-born English astronomer Caroline Herschel discovers the first of eight comets she will discover in the next 11 years.

1788 Scottish engineer William Symington builds a steam paddleboat.

A cartoon by James Gillray expressing fears that cowpox inoculation would make people look like cows.

Using Cowpox to Prevent Smallpox

The solution was eventually found by Edward Jenner (1749–1823). Jenner was the son of a clergyman and a practicing physician in the county of Gloucestershire in England. He was also an enthusiastic investigator of all types of nature and science—he wrote one of the most important books on the cuckoo and how it used other birds' nests, for example.

TIMELINE
1789-1791

KEY:

Biology and Medicine

Engineering and Invention

Chemistry and Physics

1789 German chemist Martin Klaproth discovers uranium and zirconium.

1789

1789 English clergyman Gilbert White publishes *The Natural History and Antiquities of Selborne*, a wildlife guide that is still read today.

1789 French physician Joseph Guillotin invents the guillotine, which is used from 1792 for executions during the French Revolution.

Jenner, in common with some other doctors in the late 1700s, saw that people who caught a disease called cowpox (the disease was caught from cows) developed blisters, much like smallpox blisters but less severe. However, they did not develop the more dangerous disease. Jenner realized that the pus in the cowpox blisters was protecting people against developing smallpox.

The World's First Vaccine

In 1796, Jenner tested out his theory on an eight-year-old boy named James Phipps. He used pus from the blisters of a dairymaid with cowpox and rubbed it into scratches on Phipps' arms. He then inoculated Phipps in both arms. Phipps did not develop smallpox. Jenner tried his theory on 23 other people, including his own young son, and none of them developed full-blown smallpox.

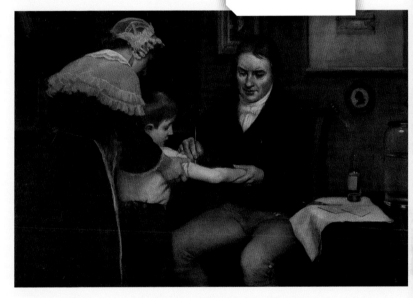

A painting of Jenner inoculating James Phipps in May 1796.

Jenner's work was recognized as being of great importance. He received worldwide recognition and many awards and honors.

1790 Claude and Ignace Chappe, from France, invent a telegraph that uses two movable arms to signal letters of the alphabet.

1791 French mineralogist Déodat de Dolomieu discovers the mineral dolomite.

1790

1791

1790 French chemist Nicolas Leblanc invents a process for making soda (calcium carbonate) from salt.

1791 William Gregor, a vicar in England, discovers titanium.

Railroads

Railroads had their origins in the 16th century, when miners in Europe used horses to pull wagons along "roads" of timber beams laid lengthwise on the ground.

A locomotive crosses a boggy region west of Manchester in northern England.

TIMELINE
1792–1795

KEY:

Biology and Medicine

Engineering and Invention

Astronomy and Math

1792 Scottish engineer William Murdock uses coal gas for domestic lighting.

1793 The remains of a mammoth are discovered preserved in permafrost in Siberia.

1792

1793

1793 French naturalist Jean-Baptiste Lamarck reintroduces the theory that fossils are the remains of extinct plants and animals.

1793 U.S. engineer Eli Whitney invents the cotton gin, which separates the seeds from cotton fibers.

A postage stamp showing Trevithick's locomotive.

In the 16th and 17th centuries, miners in Europe used trucks on wooden rails to move coal. When Abraham Darby began making cheap cast iron in the early 1700s, stronger cast-iron rails became available.

Steam Enters the Scene

The first steam locomotive was built in 1803 by English engineer Richard Trevithick. The locomotive and rolling stock had unflanged wheels, but there was a lip on the outer edge of the track. Four years later, he built a circular track in London and charged people to ride on his train—which was called Catch Me Who Can.

This drawing shows the opening of the Stockton & Darlington Railway in 1825.

The first railroad to regularly carry passengers as well as freight opened in 1825. With locomotives built by English engineer George Stephenson, the Stockton & Darlington Railway ran for 26 miles (42 km). The first intercity line, the Liverpool & Manchester Railway, opened in 1830, and the first train was hauled by Stephenson's Rocket. Built mainly to carry cotton from the port of Liverpool to the mills in

1795 France introduces the metric system of measuring using base 10.

1795 Scottish geologist James Hutton publishes his ideas on the history of Earth, which form the basis of modern geology.

1795

1795 French astronomer Joseph de Lalande observes Neptune but does not recognize it as a new planet.

1795 English inventor Joseph Bramah invents a hydraulic press.

Stephenson's Rocket

The most famous early locomotive was the Rocket, built by George Stephenson. Rocket improved on earlier models and set the pattern for all later steam trains. Some people were worried that passengers would not be able to breathe in the rushing air.

The Rocket won trials to become the locomotive on the first intercity line.

Manchester in the northwest of England, the line had to cross an extensive bog. Stephenson (who was also the railroad's chief construction engineer) overcame the problem by building it on compacted hurdles "floating" on the waterlogged ground.

Railroads also sprang up in other countries. In the United States, the year 1830 saw the inauguration of the Baltimore & Ohio Railroad, which initially ran for 13 miles (21 km) from Baltimore to Ellicott's Mills. The South Carolina Railroad opened in 1831, and was the longest railroad in the world at the time. It ran for 154 miles (248 km) from Charleston to Hamburg. France and Germany got their first railroads in 1832 and 1835, respectively. By 1840, there were railroads in Austria, Ireland, and the Netherlands. As the new railroads appeared, barges disappeared and canals fell into disrepair.

TIMELINE
1796–1800

KEY:

Biology and Medicine

Astronomy and Math

Chemistry and Physics

1796 French astronomer Pierre-Simon de Laplace suggests that the sun and planets condensed out of a swirling mass of gas.

1796

1797

1796 German physician Franz Gall introduces phrenology, which relates mental ability to the shape of the head—the theory is now discounted.

1797 The mineral chromium is discovered, followed by strontium in 1798.

The Liverpool & Manchester Railway carried freight as well as passengers.

Changing the Tracks

As well as locomotives and rolling stock, railroads need other equipment. The "road" of the original railroads employed iron rails. They were made of cast iron, at first with a right-angled section to keep the wheels on the track. Soon, these flanged rails were replaced. The flanges were put on the wheels of the vehicles, which ran on short "fish-bellied" rails that were straight on top but curved beneath to make them thicker (and stronger) in the center. From 1858, cast iron was replaced by steel.

As chief engineer of the Liverpool & Manchester Railway, George Stephenson was also responsible for designing and building structures such as this tunnel.

Railroad switches were invented as early as 1789 for tramway systems. As soon as trains started running into each other, signals were invented. They took the form of disks or arms that rotated or pivoted. In 1849, the New York and Erie Company introduced block signaling, which does not allow a train to enter a section of track until the previous train has left it. Eventually, block signals were linked electrically. Within a few decades, railroads would link vast distances.

1798 English economist Thomas Malthus discovers a relationship between the size of a population and the available food supply—the former always increases more quickly than the latter.

1799 English scientists Thomas Beddoes and Humphry Davy conduct experiments using laughing gas (nitrous oxide).

1798

1799

1800

1798 Danish mathematician Caspar Wessel represents complex numbers as vectors (quantities with magnitude and direction).

1799 American-born British scientist Benjamin Thompson helps found the Royal Institution in London.

1800 English astronomer William Herschel discovers infrared radiation (from the sun).

Glossary

bellows A flexible air chamber that is pumped to create a stream of air to produce a draught for a fire or furnace.

cast iron A type of iron containing a lot of carbon, which is too hard to be shaped and so is molded, or cast, in the shape required.

chronometer An extremely accurate mechanical clock, used for finding ships' longitude at sea.

comet A small, icy body in orbit around the sun.

element Any substance that cannot be split chemically into simpler substances.

flange A projecting rim that sticks out from a roller or rail to act as a guide.

furnace An enclosed chamber in which fire is used to produce very high temperatures for smelting metals.

governor A mechanical device that automatically regulates the speed of a machine.

horsepower A measurement of power, originally developed by James Watt to measure the power of steam engines against that of draft horses.

latitude The distance of a point on the globe north or south of the equator, measured as an angle.

lightning conductor A metal rod placed on top of a tall structure to protect it by attracting lightning strikes and carrying the charge harmlessly to the ground.

lock A stretch of a canal enclosed by gates to control the water level and raise or lower boats passing through it.

longitude The distance of a point on the globe east or west of the prime meridian, measured as an angle.

meridian An imaginary line of longitude that circles Earth from the North to the South Pole; the prime meridian, or 0°, passes through Greenwich, England.

reaping The process of cutting a crop in order to harvest it.

rolling stock The carriages and wagons pulled by a locomotive.

treadle A foot-operated rocker that drives mechanical motion.

vacuum A completely empty space in which there are no atoms or molecules of any substance.

variolation The deliberate infection with smallpox to immunize against the disease.

Further Information

Books

Allen, Robert C. *The Industrial Revolution: A Very Short Introduction*. Very Short Introductions, 2017.

Biesty, Stephen and Richard Platt. *Cross Sections Man-of-War*. Dorling Kindersley, 2019.

Captivating History. *The Industrial Revolution: A Captivating Guide to a Period of Major Industrialization*. Captivating History, 2020.

Coulis, Anthony. *Stationary Steam Engines*. Amberley Publishing, 2019.

O'Neill, Bill. *Amazing Inventions That Changed the World*. LAK Publishing 2022.

Paris, John Ayrton. *The Life of Sir Humphrey Davy*. Legare Street Press, 2022.

Priestley, Joseph. *Memoirs of Dr Joseph Priestly*, Sunbury Press, 2022.

Rooney, Anne. *The History of Astronomy (The History of Science)*. Rosen Publishing, 2018.

Woods, Michael and Mary B. Woods. *Machines Through the Ages. From Furnaces to Factories (Technology Through the Ages)*. Lerner Publishing Group, 2024.

Websites

www.bbc.co.uk/bitesize/articles/z6kg3j6#zsqk4xs
Video about the Industrial Revolution, with case studies on major people and inventions that shaped the modern world.

www.biography.com/political-figures/benjamin-franklin
Biography, inventions, and quick facts about Benjamin Franklin.

www.history.com/topics/industrial-revolution/industrial-revolution
History.com pages with photographs and links about the Industrial Revolution and the scientific developments that took place.

www.khanacademy.org/humanities/big-history-project/acceleration/bhp-acceleration/a/the-industrial-revolution
Article on fossil fuels, steam power, and the rise of manufacturing in the 18th century.

Index